SPORTS BRANDS

LULULEMON ATHLETICA

BY RACQUEL FORAN

Content Consultant
Professor John Meindl
Lecturer, Sport Management
Farmingdale State College (SUNY)

Essential Library
An Imprint of Abdo Publishing
abdobooks.com

ABDOBOOKS.COM

Published by Abdo Publishing, a division of ABDO, PO Box 398166, Minneapolis, Minnesota 55439. Copyright © 2023 by Abdo Consulting Group, Inc. International copyrights reserved in all countries. No part of this book may be reproduced in any form without written permission from the publisher. Essential Library™ is a trademark and logo of Abdo Publishing.

Printed in the United States of America, North Mankato, Minnesota.
052022
092022

THIS BOOK CONTAINS RECYCLED MATERIALS

Cover Photo: Nicky J Sims/Getty Images Entertainment/Getty Images
Interior Photos: Shutterstock Images, 4–5, 6–7, 22, 33, 49, 63, 71, 96; Jonathan Weiss/Shutterstock Images, 11; Andrey Burmakin/Shutterstock Images, 12–13; Dmytro Vietrov/Shutterstock Images, 16–17; Ben Nelms/Reuters/Alamy, 20; Lucky Business/Shutterstock Images, 23; Joe Raedle/Getty Images News/Getty Images, 24–25; iStockphoto, 26, 93; Mary Altaffer/AP Images, 34–35; Tim P. Whitby/Getty Images Entertainment/Getty Images, 38; Steven Senne/AP Images, 41; Chris Allan/Shutterstock Images, 44–45; Andrew Chin/Getty Images Entertainment/Getty Images, 46–47; Xaume Olleros/Bloomberg/Getty Images, 51, 88; Simon Dawson/Bloomberg/Getty Images, 55, 68–69; Richard Frazier/Shutterstock Images, 58–59; Stuart C. Wilson/Getty Images Entertainment/Getty Images, 60; Aaron Harris/Bloomberg/Getty Images, 66; Richard B. Levine/Alamy, 75; Jim Bennett/Getty Images Entertainment/Getty Images, 76–77; David L. Ryan/The Boston Globe/Getty Images, 81; Andrey Popov/Shutterstock Images, 90–91; Liz Hafalia/The San Francisco Chronicle/Hearst Newspapers/Getty Images, 99

Editor: Arnold Ringstad
Series Designer: Sarah Taplin

Library of Congress Control Number: 2021951740
Publisher's Cataloging-in-Publication Data
Names: Foran, Racquel, author.
Title: Lululemon Athletica / by Racquel Foran.
Description: Minneapolis, Minnesota : Abdo Publishing, 2023 | Series: Sports brands | Includes online resources and index.
Identifiers: ISBN 9781532198120 (lib. bdg.) | ISBN 9781098271770 (ebook)
Subjects: LCSH: Clothing and dress--Juvenile literature. | Lululemon Athletica--Juvenile literature. | Sport clothes industry--Juvenile literature. | Brand name products--Juvenile literature.
Classification: DDC 338.7--dc23

CONTENTS

CHAPTER ONE
CLOTHING MADE FOR YOGA 4

CHAPTER TWO
FUNCTIONAL FABRIC 12

CHAPTER THREE
FUNCTIONAL FASHION 24

CHAPTER FOUR
RETAIL REIMAGINED. 34

CHAPTER FIVE
MORE THAN A BRAND, A CULTURE 46

CHAPTER SIX
GROWTH AND CHANGE .58

CHAPTER SEVEN
EXPANDING PRODUCT LINES 68

CHAPTER EIGHT
CHALLENGES AND CONTROVERSIES 76

CHAPTER NINE
A BRIGHT FUTURE 90

ESSENTIAL FACTS	100	INDEX	110
GLOSSARY	102	ABOUT THE AUTHOR	112
ADDITIONAL RESOURCES	104	ABOUT THE CONSULTANT	112
SOURCE NOTES	106		

CHAPTER ONE

CLOTHING MADE FOR YOGA

Looking around the studio, Jessie was glad to see her beginner yoga class was full. More and more people were including yoga in their fitness routines. Over the years, attitudes had changed. She remembered that when she first discovered yoga, her friends thought she was weird. They said she was a hippie.

Jessie also remembered that she had to wear her running shorts and T-shirt while practicing yoga. The first time she attended a beginner class, she could barely see what the instructor was doing because his baggy sweatpants and T-shirt hid his body. Jessie's Lululemon leggings and crop top are much more practical for yoga. She glanced around and realized

> *Yoga's increasing popularity has led to a larger assortment of clothing designed especially for its practice.*

WICKING FABRIC

Wicking fabric is designed to keep sweat away from skin. Natural fibers such as cotton absorb moisture. The fabric gets sticky, heavy, smelly, and wet. Wicking fabric does not absorb moisture. It is designed to lift sweat away from the skin to the outer surface of the fabric, where it quickly evaporates, leaving both the skin and the fabric dry. Wicking fabrics are not exclusive to Lululemon. Many athletic wear manufacturers use their own similar materials. Under Armour helped create the market for wicking fabrics in sports apparel in 1996. Nike has Dri-FIT, Adidas has Climalite, and Reebok has PlayDry.

most of the class was wearing Lululemon. More people were buying clothes specifically for yoga. Jessie thought to herself how far yoga and yoga wear had come since her high school days.

Fifteen minutes into the class, Jessie was building up a sweat. She could feel it dripping down her temple. She hated the feeling of being sweaty, so she loved that her outfit wicked sweat away from her body. This was different from her old gym clothes, which would absorb sweat and become wet, smelly, and uncomfortable.

Jessie glanced at the mirror to check the alignment of her crescent lunge before she reached up toward the ceiling to hold the pose. She could see the contour of her muscles as they strained to hold the position. The snug fit of her leggings allowed

> *For yoga positions like the crescent lunge, clothing that is tight, stretchy, and flexible is ideal.*

her to check that her hip, knee, and ankle were straight. She could hold the pose comfortably without her leggings or top riding up. In the past, Jennie was constantly having to adjust her clothes during class. That was a frustration she was happy to shed when she discovered Lululemon.

As her class ended, Jessie thought about how Lululemon went beyond yoga wear. She had pursued yoga through free classes at a Lululemon store. She now owned her own yoga studio and was an ambassador for Lululemon. She felt she was part of something different—something bigger than just athletic wear. She was part of a community.

WHO IS CHIP WILSON?

Chip Wilson was born in 1955 in San Diego, California. His family moved to Calgary, Alberta, Canada, his father's hometown, when he was five years old. His father was a physical education teacher, and his mother worked from home as a seamstress. Both their vocations would influence and help Wilson in his career. He graduated from the University of Calgary in 1979. Lululemon Athletica was not Wilson's first try at sports apparel. He founded and operated Westbeach Snowboard, a skateboarding, surfing, and snowboarding apparel company that he launched in 1979 and sold in 1997.

WHAT IS LULULEMON ATHLETICA?

Lululemon Athletica was founded in 1998 in Vancouver, British Columbia, Canada, by Chip Wilson. It began as a line of yoga wear for women. What Wilson did not know then was that Lululemon would change athletic wear, reimagine retail, and shift ideas about effective marketing. In less than 25 years, Lululemon grew from what Wilson called "a pair of little black stretchy pants" dreamed up in a Vancouver neighborhood to a global brand that appears to be unstoppable.[1]

It all started with yoga. Wilson has a philosophy that if he hears something three times in a short space of time, he should act on it. In the summer of 1998, Wilson read an article about yoga, heard a group of people talking about yoga, and then saw a poster on a telephone pole for a yoga class. His instincts told him to take a yoga class.

Wilson saw that yoga was growing. Each week, the class had more participants. He also noticed that people were wearing a ragtag assortment of their oldest and ugliest clothes to work out in. The instructor's dance wear seemed too flimsy for the workout.

YOGA TREND

Chip Wilson was right when he predicted the growth of yoga. When Lululemon launched in 1998, yoga was not very popular. However, it has steadily grown in popularity since. In 2005, *Yoga Journal* magazine reported that 16.5 million people practiced yoga in the United States.[2] By 2020, Statista reported that 55 million Americans practiced yoga.[3] The number of yoga-specific styles of pants available through worldwide retailers has surpassed 10,000.[4]

Wilson also read a statistic saying that 60 percent of college graduates were women.[5] This was a significant increase since the 1970s, and Wilson saw an opportunity in a growing demographic of young, working women. All these observations led to the birth of Lululemon.

THE VISION

Wilson had unique ideas about what he wanted Lululemon to be. He did not want it to be just an apparel company. He viewed Lululemon as a social experiment. His vision for Lululemon was to "elevate the world from mediocrity to greatness."[6] This manifesto carried through to both people and product development. He believed if his staff were encouraged to grow and had the opportunity to contribute meaningfully to the company, he would have a better company. And if customer feedback drove his clothing designs, he could create the best technical athletic apparel on the market.

NAMING LULULEMON

When deciding what to name his company, Wilson presented a list of 20 name options to a focus group of women, and Lululemon was the outstanding favorite. At the time he expected the focus group would prefer Athletically Hip, which was another name on the list. Recognizing that the name Lululemon did not tell people what the company sold, he added the word Athletica as a descriptor.

> *In the span of a few decades, Lululemon has become one of the world's most popular sports brands.*

His experiment has proved to be incredibly successful. The name Lululemon is synonymous with yoga wear, but the company also makes athletic wear for runners, cyclists, and other athletes. In 2021, Lululemon had 521 retail outlets in 17 different countries and employed approximately 25,000 people globally.[7] The company did $4.4 billion in sales in 2020, with almost $600 million in profits.[8] Along the way, Lululemon has changed the world of sports apparel.

CHAPTER TWO

FUNCTIONAL FABRIC

Wilson always considered the functionality of the clothing he designed. Although he knew clothes needed to look good if people were going to wear them, he also understood the performance of the clothes was what would set his designs apart. He learned this long before he launched Lululemon.

In the late 1970s, Wilson decided he wanted to try the Ironman competition in Hawaii. The Ironman involves athletes competing in a triathlon of events. They swim 2.4 miles (3.9 km), bike 112 miles (180.3 km), and run 26.22 miles (42.2 km).[1] Athletic wear for triathletes did not exist in the 1970s. This presented a particular problem for Ironman contestants. When the athletes

▶ *The unique needs of triathletes helped inspire the development of new kinds of athletic apparel.*

WHAT ARE TECHNICAL FABRICS?

Technical fabrics are materials that serve a purpose or specific function. They were originally developed for only functional purposes, such as a firefighter's gear, where the aesthetics of the material were not as important as how it performed. Technical fabrics have improved a lot. They are often made to look good in addition to handling their functional duties. Fire-retardant pajamas, protective medical clothes, sports uniforms, waterproof jackets, and stain-resistant furniture are just a few of the everyday items that are made of technical fabrics.

transition from swimming to cycling, they do not change their clothes. The wet seams of their shorts and shirts would chafe their skin, causing painful abrasions on their thighs and underarms.

Using a stretchy fabric called Lycra, Wilson designed shorts with seams shifted away from the inside of the thigh. The result was a pair of shorts that fit, felt, and functioned like nothing before them. He sold a few pairs to cycling shops, but the demand for such athletic wear had not yet hit the mainstream. He was a little ahead of the times with his design.

In creating the shorts, though, Wilson had found and solved his first athletic wear problem. This work would ignite a lifelong passion for technical clothing that helped athletes. His Ironman shorts were the precursor to the yoga pants that would take the world by storm.

A PROBLEM WITH YOGA WEAR

In 1998, when Wilson began attending his first yoga classes in Vancouver, his apparel design juices started flowing once more. Again, he saw that the clothes people were wearing were not the best functional fit for the activity. He believed if he had to think about his clothing while engaged in an activity, it was not functioning properly. He wondered why clothing could not be comfortable and high quality but also easy to clean and care for.

Wilson learned from his yoga instructor that most instructors wore a specific brand of dance wear. Because the clothes were made for dancers, the sizes ran small. His instructor also complained about the transparency of the fabric. It would become shiny and see-through when stretched over the skin. Confident that yoga was going

QUALITY ASSURANCE

Wilson knew his line of yoga wear would be more expensive than most other athletic wear. He was sure, though, that once his customers understood how his garments were better, they would not mind paying more. He was so confident in the quality of his fabric and designs that he guaranteed customer satisfaction. If Lululemon customers are not completely satisfied with a purchase, or if the product does not live up to the company's quality standards, Lululemon gives a full refund. It does, however, qualify its return policy by saying it will not offer a refund for a product that has outlived its "practical lifetime."[2]

> *Wilson's experience with snowboarding apparel at Westbeach Snowboard played a role in his development of an ideal fabric for yoga wear.*

to be the next fitness trend, Wilson felt this was another apparel problem that needed to be solved. He thought if he could create a fabric that was soft, had antiodor and moisture-wicking properties, and was thick enough to solve the transparency problem, he could create what he considered the perfect yoga pants.

Developing technical fabric is expensive, and Wilson knew his pants would not be cheap. He asked his yoga

instructor if she would pay triple the price for better yoga wear. When she said yes, Wilson knew he was onto something.

ENGINEERING FABRIC

Before Lululemon, Wilson owned Westbeach Snowboard, a skate, surf, and snowboard apparel company. During his time at Westbeach, he discovered a fabric he felt would work well for his yoga pants. He had originally used it as a first layer under snowboard clothes for the emerging market of young female snowboarders. It was a synthetic fabric, but Wilson loved its soft, cottony feel, and he also liked that he could apply technical properties to it to manage odor and wick away moisture. The fabric was not perfect. It was too thick and shrank too much, but it was a good place to start.

    Wilson spent six months developing the fabric for his first line of yoga wear. At the time, athletic wear generally shrank and lost its shape after a few washes. He wanted his clothes to look and feel as good at five years old as they did when they were brand-new. He worked with the fabric mills to get the weight of the fabric just right. It would be lighter than what he used for the snowboarding apparel but heavier than dance wear. He also worked to perfect the technical wicking, cooling, and antiodor aspects of the fabric. To address the see-through problem, he cut the patterns extra wide, using more fabric than usual. This meant that when the fabric stretched, it did not become transparent. And finally, he determined the only way to ensure no additional shrinkage after customers bought a product was to put every garment through a hot wash and hot dryer before he sold it to the customer. The costs of material and manufacturing meant the fabric was expensive, so initially he could afford to purchase it only in black. A few years later, Lululemon trademarked the fabric under the name Luon.

Wilson also wanted to address the problem of uncomfortable seams. Not much had changed since he designed his Ironman shorts. He came across seams in all kinds of athletic wear that were uncomfortable and itchy and caused chafing. Wilson had read about a new way to construct garments. Two pieces of fabric could be joined and sewn together with a flat seam. This eliminated the need for an interior seam. Wilson saw this as the solution to the chafing problem.

With his fabric ready and his seam problem solved, Wilson bought two specialty flatlock sewing machines at the cost of $80,000 to start making samples.[3] The machines dramatically reduced the time to make a pair of pants, which cut labor costs. His next step was to make prototypes for women to try on and test.

LULULEMON'S TRADEMARKED FABRICS

Luon is Lululemon's signature fabric. It is a combination of 86 percent nylon and 14 percent Lycra.[4] It was the first fabric innovation for Lululemon. As the company expanded into athletic wear for other sports, its selection of fabrics expanded too. Luxtreme, Nulux, Nulu, Everlux, Silverescent, SenseKnit, and Ultralu are some of the high-performance fabrics that Lululemon has developed. Each has been specially engineered for comfort and performance.

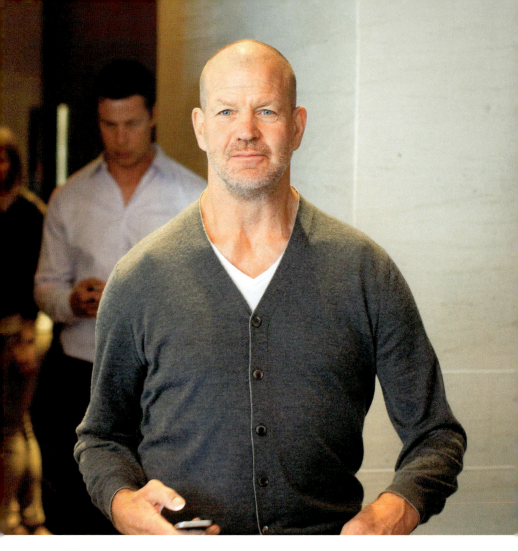

> *Wilson engaged with the local yoga community to test his new products and spread the word about the brand.*

These prototypes were brought to local yoga studios for instructors to try. As the instructors' enthusiasm for the pants grew, Wilson started supplying the studios with product to sell to those who took their classes.

Wilson initially made samples at his kitchen table. Soon he had a small but loyal customer base that was excited about his products. Encouraged, he opened his first retail store in a second-floor location that he also used as his design lab and sewing factory. In time, the popularity of his products grew to where he had to find an apparel factory that could make large quantities of clothes. He turned to some old friends, Frankie and Elky Hon, whom he worked with when he owned Westbeach. The Hons could deliver product faster than an overseas supplier because they were local. This allowed Wilson to order more inventory and restock quickly if an item was popular. The Hons eventually expanded their operation and formed a company called Charter Link. It was Lululemon's primary apparel factory for several years. Lululemon even owned 50 percent of Charter Link for a few years.[5]

THE LOGO

Like the company's name, Lululemon's logo was selected by a focus group. The stylized *A* was originally designed to fit with the name Athletically Hip, one of 20 name options under consideration. It was a coincidence that the focus group chose the stylized *A* for the logo because the word *Athletica* was not part of the company name when they chose it. The group simply liked the logo. Originally the Lululemon logo was one inch (2.5 cm) tall and appeared on the front of clothing. Eventually it became smaller—half an inch (1.3 cm) tall—and it was placed on the back of clothing. Adhering to Wilson's eye for functionality, it is also reflective.

SPORTS FOCUS

YOGA

Yoga is a physical and mental practice that originated in ancient India. It can be traced back more than 5,000 years. The word *yoga* comes from the Sanskrit word *yuj*, which means union or to join. The purpose of yoga is to connect mind, body, and spirit. All forms of yoga include physical poses, breathing, and concentration or meditation.

Because the art of yoga requires complex body movements, some kinds of clothing are too restrictive to wear for yoga. And some forms of specialized yoga, like Bikram, which is performed in heated rooms with high humidity, can make you sweat a lot. Lululemon's clothes are specifically

designed to function for yoga. In addition to the technical features of the fabric, such as wicking, antiodor properties, and breathability, Lululemon's clothes fit for yoga. Its pants are snug, so the fabric does not impede movements. The fabric is soft. There are no rough edges, buttons, zippers, or snaps. There is nothing that can dig into skin or suddenly pop open. Tops do not ride up, and pants do not slip down when reaching and bending.

Some credit Lululemon for the surge in popularity of yoga. With yoga's rising popularity, the practice's purpose began to change. Modern yoga often focuses more on exercise, strength, and balance than meditative and spiritual aspects. Regardless of how or why people practice, Lululemon developed clothing ideal for yoga's physical movements.

CHAPTER THREE

FUNCTIONAL FASHION

F inding fashion designers interested in the technical aspects of clothing design was not easy. Clothing design is all about what you can see, while technical athletic wear is all about what you cannot see. Wilson reached out to a designer he worked with at Westbeach, Amanda Dunsmoor, to help bring his vision to life.

Dunsmoor was the designer, but Wilson knew what he wanted. The design of the clothes was as important as the fabric used. Wilson gave Dunsmoor rough sketches of clothing designs, but they would include specific design elements that Wilson felt were important. Reflective spots were precisely placed, seams had to be moved away from the inner

> *To create pants meant for yoga, apparel makers must take unique design considerations into account.*

> *For many people, yoga pants have become a part of everyday casual wear.*

thigh and underarm, and the crotch of the pants was diamond-shaped with a gusset for women's comfort.

The cut of the yoga pants was different too. The waist was higher in the back than the front. This prevented the pants from riding down in the back and folding over in the front when squatting or bending down. A small flare was included at the bottom of the pants, and the outside seam was moved from the side of the leg to the back of the leg. This gave the pants a distinct look and fit. These early design elements would become signature details for Lululemon, and soon the athletic wear would move from the studio and gym to the street and cafés.

YOGA PANTS CHANGE FASHION

The first line of Lululemon products included six designs: two pairs of pants, one pair of shorts, and three tops. But it was the pants that changed everything. Wilson noticed people were starting to dress differently. It used to be that people had one set of clothes for the office, another for home, a third for exercise, and perhaps even a fourth for going out in casual settings. By the late 1990s, this was changing. Casual Fridays were common at offices. So, too, were jeans days. Men wore ties less often. Wilson had an instinct that the professional young women who were his target market would appreciate a versatile pant that they could wear at home, to the office, to exercise class, and out for coffee. They would save time if they did not have to

PANTS THAT FIT

Wilson spent a lot of time in Japan, where he learned that most retail clothing stores in the country had sewing machines so they could offer on-site tailoring. By offering free hemming, he could make pants long enough to fit tall women perfectly while still meeting the needs of women of other heights. He hired recently graduated design students to do the hemming. This gave them the opportunity to get feedback from customers while they were hemming, which they brought back to the design lab. It was one of many things that would set Lululemon apart from other retailers. The company continues to offer free hemming of its pants and tops, without requiring a receipt or proof of purchase.

change clothes, and he was sure they would pay for that convenience. It turns out he was right.

By the end of 1998, Wilson had created a small following for his new brand. People who practiced yoga knew about his product and liked it. In early 1999, he opened his first retail store, so more women learned about his comfortable and stylish pants. Then one day in 1999, Wilson saw a woman walking down the street wearing Lululemon pants. His pants had officially moved from yoga studio to street wear.

It did not take long for girls and women outside of the yoga world to start wearing Lululemon's yoga pants and leggings too. Women had rarely worn athletic or dance wear on the street before this. By 2014, only 15 years after Lululemon entered the market, a survey by investment bank Piper Jaffray reported that Lululemon-style leggings

ATHLEISURE

In 1995, Wilson tried to introduce his own new terminology to describe the intersection of street wear and technical apparel with the word *stretch*, but it did not catch on. In 1996, when he started to notice a shift from office wear to what he called street athletic, he tried again with the term *streetnic*, but that did not stick either. The term *athleisure* emerged from the New York fashion scene in 2014 to describe the fusion of athletic wear and street wear. Wilson is not a fan of the word, as he does not feel it conveys Lululemon's brand. But like it or not, Lululemon's yoga pants are largely responsible for the growth of what has become known as the athleisure market.

BOOGIE PANT

PRODUCT SPOTLIGHT

Lululemon's first yoga pant was a Lycra flare fit. Featuring Lululemon's signature elements—including flat seams, a triangle-shaped gusseted crotch, and an exterior leg seam shifted toward the back—it was a fashion game changer. Wilson named it the Boogie Pant because it reminded him of the 1970s. In 2017, the Museum of Modern Art (MoMA) in New York City held its first exhibition on fashion and design in 73 years, "Items: Is Fashion Modern?" The Boogie Pant was among the 111 pieces selected to have had a "profound effect on the world over the last century."[1]

In a 2017 interview with a Vancouver media outlet, Wilson explained why he developed the yoga pant and what made it different: "I designed the Boogie Pant to reflect the needs of Vancouver women and to enable them to move through their entire day in one garment. The pants had triple the stretch of any other pants on the market and felt like cotton instead of plastic. I added the wide-paneled gusset, which is what took the pants from the dance class to the street. They didn't shrink, and they were designed to last 10 years. They were technical made beautiful."[2]

PRODUCT SPOTLIGHT

WUNDER UNDERS

If the Boogie Pant put Lululemon on the map, Wunder Unders catapulted the brand across the globe. Unlike the Boogie Pant, Wunder Unders are leggings that fit snug to the leg. Designed based on customer feedback, Lululemon's Wunder Unders give support all over. They feature a wide, smooth waistband that hugs the core without digging in. Fashion blogs and magazines praised the Wunder Unders. Designed intentionally for yoga and training—with support and stretchability for squatting—they also feature technical aspects such as low friction, breathability, and sweat wicking.

Wunder Unders introduced Lululemon to a new target market, teenage girls. The popularity of Lululemon soared among teens, ranking as the number six brand in Piper Jaffray's 2020 Taking Stock with Teens survey.[3] Wunder Unders frequently appear in fashion lists of Lululemon's best items, and they are consistently one of Lululemon's top sellers.

were the top fashion trend for teens that year.[4] By 2016, yoga pants had become so popular that businesses were developing policies around whether they were appropriate office attire. And in 2017, US imports of women's elastic stretch pants surpassed those of blue jeans for the first time.[5] With Lululemon's help, yoga pants and leggings became a fashion standard.

MORE PRODUCTS, MORE R&D

In the company's early days, product development centered on focus groups and customer feedback. Wilson believed the only way to make garments people wanted to wear was to find out what they did and did not like about clothing. He had women bring pieces of athletic wear to focus groups and would ask them what they liked about the apparel and what they would change. When the company made its first prototypes, he had yoga

FROM FABRIC SCRAPS TO FABULOUS FASHION

On a visit to a sewing factory, Wilson and his wife, designer Shannon Gray, noticed that there was a lot of fabric waste. They observed one of the women in the sewing room using the ends she cut off pants as a headband to keep her hair out of her eyes. From this observation, one of the company's best-selling products, the Lululemon headband, was born. The company also found other creative ways to use scrap fabric. As one example, it was used in the drop-down waist of yoga pants, allowing for unique color variations on what were otherwise mass-produced black garments.

A DIFFERENT KIND OF PARTNER

In 1999, Wilson hired a designer named Shannon Gray. He was impressed with her qualifications. She had degrees in fine arts, education, and apparel design. But more importantly, her portfolio was the only one Wilson saw that included designs in stretch fabrics. Wilson credits Gray with making improvements to Lululemon's Groove Pant that turned it into a best seller. In April 2002, Wilson and Gray were married.

instructors try the pieces on and give him feedback. Then his designers used that feedback to improve the garment.

Wilson always thought about the functionality of the clothing Lululemon designed, but he knew his target market would also be thinking about look and feel. If women did not feel comfortable and they did not like the way they looked, they would not buy the product, no matter how functional it was.

This personal approach to product development has never changed, but the company has expanded its methods. Research and development evolved over the years to include professional athletes, scientists, equipment, and technology, all providing input and data to inform the next product design. Factors including fabric choice, seam placement, body temperature variation, and breathability are considered. Fabrics are designed and tested for durability, ensuring every garment has a long life. And every product is tested by people who

> *Shoppers at Lululemon stores can now find a wide variety of products beyond the yoga pants that gave the company its start.*

wear it while moving and sweating to ensure comfort, performance, and functionality.

Lululemon has come a long way since its first six designs. The popularity of its yoga line led to more sport-specific designs. The company's website lists four categories of products: women's, men's, accessories, and self-care. Each of these categories is broken down into dozens of subcategories, including leggings, joggers, shorts, hoodies, shirts, jackets, and more. And within each of these subcategories are multiple sport-specific designs. Pants and crop tops for yoga, shorts for running, and shirts for cycling are among the dozens of products available. Every garment has one thing in common, though. It has been engineered specifically to function in the sport for which it was designed.

CHAPTER FOUR

RETAIL REIMAGINED

From the moment Wilson started thinking about his yoga pants, he knew he wanted to sell them differently than clothing had been sold before. Most clothing manufacturers sell their products wholesale. Under this system, a company like Reebok makes its own products and then sells them to a retailer, such as Target. There is an extra step—a middleman—between the product and the customer. An alternate system is known as vertical retail. In vertical retail, the company makes its own products to sell directly to the customer from its own stores. Wilson calculated that he could make better profit margins by selling his product directly. He could also maintain better control over the supply chain, company

> *Selling its own products in its own stores gave Lululemon complete control over its customers' experience.*

finances, and product pricing. He had done some vertical retailing when he ran Westbeach Snowboard, and he was convinced this was the model he needed to follow for Lululemon to be successful.

Vertical retail was not the common model in 1998, and there were risks. There are more things to manage. Retail outlets require staff that need to be trained and paid. There are also the added expenses of leasing space and furnishing retail outlets. But Wilson wanted his stores to be more than retail spaces. He wanted them to be community hubs. He had a clear vision for the stores, just as he did for his products. People and functionality were in the front of his mind.

RETAIL OUTLETS

The first Lululemon Athletica store opened its doors in March 1999 on West 4th Avenue in the Kitsilano neighborhood of Vancouver, British Columbia. Its second-floor location was not easy to find, so people had to know where to look for it. The space had a good vibe, featuring big windows with mountain views. Wilson turned the space into an experiential one. He put a sewing lab in one part of the room, where customers could see new products being conceived on the spot. Designer

LOCATION, LOCATION, LOCATION

Amanda Dunsmoor would connect directly with customers and get feedback from them on the designs, which she could incorporate into her next design cut.

The rest of the space was split between storing inventory and displaying product. There was not a lot of money to finish the interior space. A fresh coat of white paint and inexpensive carpet were added to clean the place up. For an affordable and funky look, Wilson hung long wood dowels from the ceiling with rope and used them as clothing racks. Rolling racks were also used to display clothes, making the space flexible. Essential oil scents and mellow music in the background helped create a unique boutique vibe. All these renovations and features cost just $4,000.[1] But Wilson still needed to get people into his store to buy his clothes. This was when he introduced free yoga classes.

Lululemon's first retail location was not ideal, because it was on the second floor, accessed by a hidden, narrow doorway. However, Wilson knew the area well and was confident that the first store needed to be on West 4th Avenue in the Kitsilano neighborhood. Kits, as locals call it, has always had an alternative vibe. Across the bridge from Vancouver's downtown core and close to the beach, the neighborhood attracts a creative, university-aged, beach-going crowd. Natural health food stores, vegan restaurants, and vitamin supplement stores abound. The active, healthy, busy young women who lived in and hung out in Kitsilano were exactly who Wilson was targeting and who he was relying on to promote his yoga wear through word of mouth.

> *Lululemon has a long history of hosting yoga classes, both in its stores and in local communities.*

The clothes that were displayed on rolling racks could be pushed aside when the store closed. This created a perfect space to hold yoga classes. Wilson reached out to his yoga instructor, Fiona Stang, and asked her to teach the classes. She was one of only a few yoga instructors in Vancouver at the time. People followed her to the Lululemon location. When they discovered that specialty yoga clothes were also sold there, they started telling friends. Lululemon's powerful, grassroots, word-of-mouth marketing campaign began. It was a new approach to apparel design, retail sales, and marketing.

Within a year, it was clear Lululemon needed a better retail space. In November 2000, the store moved to a new ground-level unit across the street from its first location. Again, Wilson had to be creative with the space. It was too large for what was initially needed, so he built rolling walls that enabled the rooms to be moved and adjusted in size. It was an interactive space that adapted to the needs of the customers.

Lululemon's first expansion store opened on Queen Street West in Toronto, Ontario, Canada, in February 2002. The company introduced the brand to local yoga studios before the store opened. Using this same successful preopening marketing model as with the first location, the store was an immediate success. Seeing this model work in Toronto as it had in Vancouver gave Wilson confidence that his expansion model could work anywhere.

FREE YOGA CLASSES

One of the things that differentiated Lululemon from other retailers was free yoga classes for customers. Wilson initially introduced them to bring traffic to his hidden first location. Over time, the classes became as important a part of Lululemon as its yoga pants. Every week in all Lululemon stores, staff push aside product to make room for yoga mats and free yoga sessions. This offering now extends to the company's website, where customers can find a large selection of free virtual classes led by qualified instructors.

FREE POP-UP SHOP FOR RUNNERS

In September 2018, Lululemon reached out to marathon runners in New York City and Chicago, Illinois, with their "Run Stop Shop" digital vending machines. Located in highly visible areas during marathon season, the machines were stocked with all kinds of products for runners, including water, energy gels, electrolyte tablets, first aid kits, sunscreen, and antichafe butter. There were also Lululemon hats, socks, and hair ties. All the products were free. Users were asked to provide an email address and post images of themselves on social media with the hashtags #thesweatlifeNYC or #thesweatlifeCHI.

Additional stores opened in Canada in 2002. First Wilson's cousin opened a store in Calgary, Alberta. Then his wife's sister opened one in Victoria, British Columbia.

With four stores now operating and turning profits, Wilson felt ready to open a second Vancouver location. On a drizzly October morning in 2002, Wilson opened the first athletic wear store on Vancouver's extremely expensive Robson Street, a shopping corridor known for designer brands. Landlords on Robson Street charged some of the highest monthly retail rental rates in the world. To attract attention to the opening, Wilson announced that the first 30 customers to show up naked would get free Lululemon clothes. People started lining up outside the store at four o'clock in the morning, naked except for their coats. Both the publicity stunt and new store were risks that paid off. Over the next year,

Yoga's increasing popularity helped Lululemon grow rapidly in the early 2000s.

Lululemon added six more stores in Canada. Wilson was now ready to expand to the United States.

Despite having many similarities to Canada, the US market is different in many ways. In 2003, the first Lululemon store south of the border opened in Santa Monica, California, but it was not the instant success the Canadian stores had been. The company relied on its proven formula of reaching out to the local yoga community. And just as it had in Canada, slowly this approach to marketing paid off. Two more California stores opened within a year, and Lululemon officially had its foot in the US retail market. In 2011, *Forbes* magazine placed Lululemon Athletica in the thirteenth spot on its

Fastest Growing Companies list.[2] By 2012, there were 108 Lululemon stores in 28 different states.[3] That number had almost tripled by 2021, with 315 stores in the United States.[4]

All this has been achieved without relying on traditional advertising as much as most apparel companies do. Lululemon's primary marketing tool has always been grassroots connections at a community level. It hosted events and promoted them through press releases and media coverage, not advertising. When social media entered the scene, the company used this new tool as another way to engage with its customers directly. It was not until 2017 that Lululemon ran its first television ad campaign. It continues, however, to advertise less than most other athletic wear companies.

FUNCTIONAL SPACES

Wilson gave the same attention to functionality in his retail spaces as in the clothes Lululemon designed. He did not display clothes in the traditional way. Instead of organizing products in color blocks or as coordinated items to create outfits, he grouped similar things together. Pants were all on one wall, shorts were in a separate area, and shirts were grouped together. Then they were clearly labeled for purpose and hung or stacked by size. This made it easier for customers to find what they were looking for.

Changing rooms in Lululemon stores are well lit. They also have triple mirrors so customers can see how they look from all angles without having to leave the changing room. And Lululemon staff are on hand to educate customers about what items best suit their needs, but they are instructed never to upsell or give compliments about looks. Store managers are treated like entrepreneurs and are encouraged to stage their stores to fit the mood, style, and environment of their community. All Lululemon stores have a similar vibe, but none are exactly the same.

Lululemon also manages product inventory differently than other stores. It experiments with design capsules,

EXPERIENTIAL STORES

Lululemon opened its largest retail location to date in the Lincoln Park neighborhood of Chicago in July 2019. Dominating a corner location, the 20,000-square-foot (1,860 sq m) store is much more than a retail outlet. Lululemon calls the space an "experiential store" where people can "shop, workout, dine, meditate, lounge—this is the space for you to be your best."[5] In addition to retail space that offers the same services as all their locations, it includes a restaurant, lounge and workspace, meditation area, fitness studios, showers, and towel service. It also offers daily meditation and yoga classes. In November 2019, a second experiential store opened at the Mall of America in Bloomington, Minnesota.

> *Lululemon stores in different locations have their own unique looks.*

where it introduces a new product in limited numbers to test feedback and popularity. The company also makes relatively few numbers of its designs, resulting in larger demand than supply. Customers know they must buy a product when they see it because it probably will not be there the next time they visit. This generates excitement around new apparel releases, ensures rapid turnover of products, reduces overstock problems, and eliminates the need to mark down items.

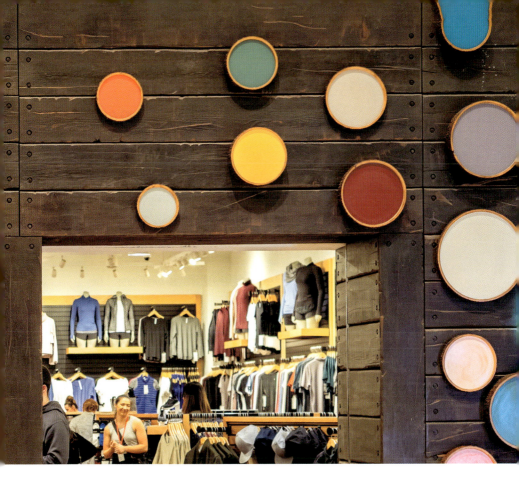

Lululemon's community-based, vertical retail model has proven to be very successful. Its stores have a fast turnover of goods, with new products coming out more frequently than in many other apparel stores. In 2017, it had among the highest retail sales per square foot in the United States at $1,560.[6] In comparison, in 2020 the high-end department store Nordstrom earned $303 per square foot.[7]

CHAPTER FIVE

MORE THAN A BRAND, A CULTURE

Chip Wilson had unconventional ideas about how he wanted to develop Lululemon and the people who worked for it. He also knew who its target customers were and how he wanted Lululemon to influence them. He wanted to do more than sell athletic wear to people. He said he sought to improve people's lives. Lululemon's mission statement is, "Providing components for people to live a longer, healthier, and more fun life."[1] The company manifesto says Lululemon's goal is "elevating the world from mediocrity to greatness."[2] These ideas inform the company's decisions, from designing clothes and stores to hiring, training, and developing staff. This culture also guides customer engagement.

> *Chip Wilson, second from right, and other members of Lululemon's corporate leadership team appear at the opening of the flagship store in Vancouver in 2014.*

For Wilson, maintaining Lululemon's culture meant employees had to share the same vision, values, and corporate language.

LEADERSHIP DEVELOPMENT

Lululemon was a small team in the beginning. Wilson had to trust his instincts about the people he hired. It started with only Wilson and designer Amanda Dunsmoor. Shannon Gray and Jackie Slater joined the team as designers in 1999. When finances were tight, Wilson went back to work for Westbeach, the company he had sold. He took Dunsmoor with him. Wilson trusted Gray and Slater to run Lululemon alone during this time.

It was with Gray and Slater that Wilson began to formalize the company's culture and ideas for employee development. This started with having the two women listen to the self-help audiobook *The Psychology of Achievement* by Brian Tracy. Wilson then instructed them to have anyone they hired also listen to the tapes. Eventually, attending a personal development program called the Landmark Forum and reading several other books were added to company training. Wilson believed the insights found in these materials transformed people, making them into leaders and helping them raise up

> *Lululemon's leadership training was designed to give new employees the ability to successfully run a new store, helping to grow and expand the brand in the process.*

the people around them. With Lululemon's training, he wanted to know he could send someone in their early twenties to a new city to run a store and be confident that person would be able to do so with integrity, responsibility, and creativity.

Goal setting plays a big role in the culture at Lululemon. Staff are asked to envision a ten-year plan for their lives and then set specific attainable goals to achieve that vision. The goals are divided into family, career, and health. Wilson believed adding this element to staff training elevated Lululemon beyond an apparel company to a leadership development company. Staff are encouraged to use the leadership skills they learn working at Lululemon to pursue and achieve goals outside the company, even pursuits that include leaving the company.

Wilson felt it was important that everyone in the company not only had the same standards but also communicated in the same way. He wanted to be confident that someone working in Vancouver could communicate just as effectively with a coworker in the next room as they could with a supplier in China. Wilson called these terms "linguistic abstractions." There were between 20 and 30 of these business terms that were used universally across the company. Examples include "committed listening," which was defined as paying attention to both verbal and nonverbal cues when listening and understanding that by listening you are not committing to act. A "by-when date" was the time or date by which a person promised to complete a project or task. And a "condition of satisfaction" referred to the criteria by which a completed promise could be measured.[3] Wilson believed well-developed employees who all understood the same corporate language would help the company grow and prosper.

> *Wilson wanted Lululemon employees to take on the responsibility of teaching customers about all the products the company has to offer.*

EDUCATING BEFORE SELLING

Wilson took a new approach to selling. He was committed to growing Lululemon through word of mouth at the community level. He was driven first by providing health and athletic information to his customers, whom he called guests. He believed that if they bought something and were satisfied with the experience, they would return to buy more.

Wilson also knew Lululemon had higher prices than competing brands. He would have to educate his customers about the clothes so they would understand their value. Lululemon calls its front-end retail staff Educators. In his book, Wilson noted that the number one principle of Lululemon is "the store Educator is the most important person in the business, and all decisions are made with this in mind."[4] Educators are trained to focus not on increasing sales but instead on educating guests. Educators are meant to help customers find what fits their needs, even if it means sending them to a competitor, such as Nike or Adidas. Having staff focused on educating and helping customers—not solely on selling them products—along with a corporate culture that encourages personal growth and development reflects Wilson's stated objective to put people before profits. It also helped differentiate Lululemon from its competitors.

COMMUNITY AND CUSTOMERS

Lululemon's culture extends beyond its management and staff to its customers and the community it serves. From its early days in its hidden second-floor location, Lululemon's grassroots approach to selling its products helped build customer loyalty. Customers who shopped at Lululemon stores noticed and appreciated the difference. Having Lululemon staff educate them about products as well as ask for their feedback on the clothes made customers feel like they were part of the design process. Motivational quotes on chalkboards and shopping bags made customers feel like Lululemon was rooting for them, encouraging them to lead healthier, more active lives. And offering people bonuses such as free yoga and meditation classes, free reusable bags, and free pant hemming set Lululemon apart from other retailers and helped build more brand loyalty.

SKIRTING THE RULES

Lululemon has often taken a tongue-in-cheek approach with its marketing. This was on clear display leading up to the 2010 Winter Olympics in Vancouver. The company saw a moneymaking opportunity with such a huge athletic event taking place in its own backyard. However, the International Olympic Committee (IOC) has strict copyright restrictions. No company is permitted to use the word *Olympics* or an assortment of related words and phrases unless it is an authorized sponsor or supplier. Despite this, Lululemon still released a line of clothes to mark the event. It worked around the restrictions by calling the line the "Cool Sporting Event That Takes Place in British Columbia Between 2009 and 2011 Edition."[5]

    Lululemon also marketed itself differently, at first because it did not have the money to pay for expensive advertising but then because its community-based approach proved to be effective. Celebrities, expensive music rights, and flashy television ads have never been part of the company's marketing arsenal. It built brand awareness and brand loyalty one customer at a time

AMBASSADOR PROGRAM

Wilson relied heavily on yoga instructors to test and promote his clothes, so he formalized agreements with them by providing them with new designs in exchange for their feedback in design meetings. Eventually, this grew to become the ambassador program. An array of athletes, including yoga instructors, snowboarders, surfers, boxers, runners, dancers, skiers, and cyclists now wear and promote Lululemon athletic wear. In addition to free athletic wear, ambassadors gain access to mentoring and networking.

through community yoga classes, store ambassadors, and word of mouth.

Lululemon has continued to use community outreach to grow its brand recognition, but it now also uses social media to take this outreach to the next level. Programs such as Sweat Collective and Lululemon Collective connect the brand with a broader audience of athletes. Lululemon describes the Sweat Collective as "an inspiring community of the world's sweatiest leaders." The company encourages "leaders in sweat" to apply for the program.[6] If accepted, members of the Sweat Collective are offered Lululemon perks and benefits. They are also asked for feedback on products. Eligible applicants include fitness instructors, personal trainers, athletes, coaches, and studio owners and managers.

The Lululemon Collective is a similar program but targeted at people who live "the sweat life."[7] These are

> *Classes, programs, and other forms of community outreach have helped Lululemon gain many dedicated customers and fans.*

Sweat with u

THURS @ 6 45 PM

BACKPACKERS RUN

SAT @ 9 00 AM

HIIT WITH IZZY

SUN @ 10 30 AM

TRIYOGA X LULUL

#THESWEATLIFE ONLINE COMMUNITY

Lululemon's website does more than sell yoga wear. It is also an extension of the company's culture. The website offers free resources for anyone looking to improve their physical or mental health. Lululemon describes its #thesweatlife online community as a "hub for your sweat sessions and mindfulness practices—wherever you are."[9] A large selection of video classes is available to watch, with topics including yoga, meditation, mindfulness, stretching, core conditioning, and full-body workouts. Classes are typically 25 to 35 minutes long and are led by Lululemon ambassadors. active people who are not fitness professionals or leaders. Members of the Lululemon Collective become affiliate influencers. They promote Lululemon through their social media feeds, and then they get a commission on any sales generated from their posts.

Through the company's website, Lululemon provides other ways for people to engage with the brand while pursuing their own fitness goals. There are running groups, in-store yoga sessions, online classes, and social media groups to keep the Lululemon community active. In 2018, the company hosted more than 4,000 community events.[8] Community engagement has proven to be a very successful way to attract and maintain loyal customers.

Another way Lululemon has set itself apart is with its manifesto, a set of quotes that sums up the company's values. The manifesto has played a key role in how the company has branded itself. Printed on its bags, the manifesto was used to connect Lululemon customers

SHOPPING BAG REVOLUTION

to the company's culture of an active, healthy lifestyle. The most controversial of the manifesto quotes was, "Coke, Pepsi, and other pops will be known as the cigarettes of the future. Colas are not a substitute for water. Colas are just another cheap drug made to look great by advertising." Wilson was adamant that people know what Lululemon stood for and did not back down from including this on its bags. Quotes in the Manifesto printed on the original 2003

Lululemon's shopping bags are almost as well known as its yoga pants. The company was among the first retailers to offer reusable, recyclable shopping bags. In the first store, Wilson would share inspiring sayings with customers and staff. This morphed into Lululemon's manifesto, an instantly recognizable branding tool. Wilson hired some graphic artists from the surf and snowboard scene to turn this list of thoughts and observations into art. He had the artistic layout of words printed on bags. By 2003, Lululemon bags were seen all over the streets of Vancouver. They were being used and reused by men, women, and children to carry everything from running shoes and gym wear to lunch and groceries.

bag included, "Love," and, "Do yoga. It lets you live in the moment and stretching releases toxins from your muscles." Another was, "Your outlook on life is a direct reflection of how much you like yourself." Manifesto quotes also included, "Do one thing a day that scares you," "Friends are more important than money," and, "Dance, sing, floss, travel."[10]

CHAPTER SIX

GROWTH AND CHANGE

By 2004, Lululemon was making a name for itself in the apparel industry. Wilson received a letter from lingerie company Victoria's Secret expressing an interest in buying the company. He turned down the offer. However, it made him realize that he needed to start thinking about Lululemon's growth and his future role in the company. He knew the interest in his company meant Lululemon needed to become a bigger player in the US market or it would be swallowed by another company. Selling a portion of his company would give Lululemon the money it needed to expand, as well as provide his family with financial security.

> *Lululemon had become an enormously popular brand by the early 2000s, and Wilson had important decisions to make about the company's future.*

▶ *Lululemon sometimes holds mass yoga events to commemorate important milestones in the company's history.*

In 2005, Wilson started looking for investors. He received offers from fashion company Liz Claiborne and clothing retailer The Gap. He did not accept either because he felt the first was not a good cultural fit and the second did not offer enough money. Instead, in October 2005, he signed a deal to sell 48 percent of Lululemon for $200 million to two private equity firms.[1]

By selling a piece of Lululemon, Wilson thought he was buying experience and guidance from his new partners. He had built something amazing, but people kept telling him he knew nothing about growing a $200 million company into a billion-dollar company. Despite his success, he believed them and felt he needed outside help to bring Lululemon to the next level. The new partners ended up deciding to take the company public.

When a company goes public, it must first value itself and then determine what one share of that value is worth. The shares are then made available on the stock market for the public to purchase through an initial public offering (IPO). People who buy shares in a company become shareholders in the company. Shareholders gain voting rights in corporate decisions. Publicly owned companies also need a board of directors. Some board members are large shareholders in the company. Executives and managers run companies, but the board often votes on major corporate decisions.

On July 27, 2007, to recognize the day of its IPO, Lululemon stopped traffic in New York City's Times Square to hold a yoga event. The shares started at $18, but the price

A GOOD INVESTMENT

Lululemon Athletica has consistently performed well for investors. Those who owned $1,000 worth of shares in 2009 were almost $20,000 richer ten years later. The stock earned a 1,929 percent return on their investment.[2] Lululemon was an anomaly among retailers during the COVID-19 pandemic, continuing to pay its staff and avoiding any permanent store closures or deep markdowns. In June 2020, financial website MarketWatch rated Lululemon the top publicly traded retailer. Between November 2020 and November 2021, its share price increased from approximately $315 to $460.[3]

shot to $25 within minutes of the stock market opening. Lululemon sold 18.2 million shares, raising $327.6 million. Wilson retained 30 percent of the company.[4]

GOING GLOBAL

Lululemon was on an expansion path. The company continued to open stores across North America, but it was also expanding to overseas markets. Its first location outside North America was in Melbourne, Australia. Lululemon Chapel Street opened there in October 2004. By the end of 2007, there were five Lululemon stores in Japan too. However, the Japanese stores did not survive the worldwide financial crisis of 2008, and all were closed.

It was six years before Lululemon opened another new store overseas, and the company took a cautious approach. It relied on its proven method of community outreach to generate buzz about stores before they opened. In advance of its first European store opening, the company ran several small pop-up showrooms throughout London, England, that opened only a few days of the week. It also held public events, including a 90-minute yoga session accompanied by a live orchestra at the Royal Opera House. The first full store in Europe finally opened in London on March 28, 2014. On the day of

> *A wide selection of yoga pants is available at Lululemon's store at a Hong Kong shopping mall.*

the opening, Lululemon worked with a local yoga studio to offer free yoga classes throughout the city.

Later that year, Lululemon reentered the Asian market with small pop-up showrooms in Singapore before officially opening its first store in that country on December 14, 2014. In conjunction with the store opening, the company used several community-based initiatives to introduce Lululemon's culture to its new customer base. In partnership with local businesses, Lululemon led a pilot program that brought exercise classes to work. It also installed public art that included Lululemon's manifesto.

GLOBAL STORES

By 2021, Lululemon had stores in 17 different countries. Most were in the United States, with 315 locations spread across the country. There were 62 stores in Canada. The North American market accounted for 86 percent of Lululemon's sales in 2020. The other 144 stores were distributed across 15 countries. China had 55 stores, the most in a single country outside of North America. Australia had 31 stores.[8] CEO Calvin McDonald saw a lot of room for growth, particularly in the European and Asian markets. His goal was to achieve 50 percent of revenue from the international stores.[9]

Expansion continued at a rapid pace. By January 2018, there were 270 Lululemon stores in the United States, 57 in Canada, and 70 more located in ten other countries.[5] To help increase its global exposure, Lululemon launched new e-commerce websites in China, Japan, South Korea, Germany, and France by July 2019. In Asian countries, once again setting it apart from most clothing manufacturers, it used local models on its websites. Lululemon also adjusted its sizes to match typical local body types.

Lululemon shows no signs of slowing down. During times when many retailers struggled to keep stores open in a shifting retail landscape, Lululemon continued to open new stores. In 2020, during the global pandemic, Lululemon opened 30 new locations.[6] In 2021, the company once again made *Fortune* magazine's list of 100 Fastest Growing Companies.[7] It planned to continue opening new stores around the world.

CHANGE IN LEADERSHIP

With growth comes change. When Wilson sold 48 percent of the company, he also made the decision to hire a chief executive officer (CEO). Wilson held the title of chief innovation and branding officer, and he brought in Bob Meers to be CEO. He was counting on Meers to streamline some of Lululemon's business practices. Meers helped improve production capacity, but his executive ways did not really fit in with Lululemon's culture. Employees who had been with the company since the beginning felt he was hiring the wrong kind of people. They felt these new people did not join the company because they believed in its culture but, instead, solely to make money. For example, one former employee noted that new hires were not necessarily interested in fitness. Meers resigned shortly after Lululemon's IPO.

Meers was replaced by Christine Day. Day was at

SISTER ACT

Wilson was always on the lookout for women to join Lululemon as Educators. During the 2000 Christmas season he asked his neighbor, Deanne Schweitzer, to come and work for him. She agreed and within four weeks became Lululemon's first store manager. A year later, her sister Delaney joined the company as an Educator. Both women were promoted to top ranks in the company. Deanne worked her way up to head of product. Delaney would be promoted to run all store operations and e-commerce.

> CEO Christine Day oversaw a period of sustained financial success for Lululemon.

the helm of Lululemon from 2008 to 2013. During her time, the company's revenue grew from $350 million to $1.5 billion.[10] However, it was during her tenure that Wilson began to sense a shift in the culture of the company. He felt he was losing influence. A consulting firm was hired to review how Lululemon designed products and brought them to market. Wilson was asked to move his desk out of the design area, where it had always been. He also felt too much focus was being put on cutting costs and finding ways to increase product prices.

During this time, Wilson brought several proposals to the board of directors, suggesting new directions in which to take Lululemon, but they did not share his vision. He became increasingly frustrated with the fact that he had less power and influence than when he owned Lululemon outright. He also felt quality control was suffering for the sake of more profits. On January 29, 2012, with friction between Day, the board, and Wilson increasing, he resigned his position and stepped away from his day-to-day role at Lululemon. He remained chairman of the board until December 2013, when he resigned from this role as well. In 2014, he sold half his remaining shares to an investment firm. The next year he announced he was stepping down from the board of directors. In 2021, Wilson was still the largest single shareholder in Lululemon, owning 8 percent of company shares, but he did not play an active role with the company.[11]

LULULEMON CHIEF EXECUTIVE OFFICERS

Wilson held the position of CEO of Lululemon until late 2005, when Bob Meers was hired. Meers was previously with Reebok and had helped build it into one of the top athletic wear companies in the world. In 2008, Meers was replaced by Christine Day. Day came from Starbucks, where she had worked for more than two decades. She held the CEO position at Lululemon until 2013. Day was replaced by Laurent Potdevin, a former president of shoe company Toms, in January 2014. In a surprise announcement in February 2018, Potdevin resigned. Lululemon released a statement saying he did not "exemplify the highest levels of integrity and respect for one another."[12] It did not give specific examples of his behavior. In August 2018, Calvin McDonald, a former executive from beauty products retailer Sephora, took over as CEO.

CHAPTER SEVEN

EXPANDING PRODUCT LINES

One way Lululemon grew its customer base was by expanding its product selection. New products are how retailers bring customers back to their stores repeatedly and how they attract new customers. In the early days, Wilson added yoga mats to the line of products Lululemon sold. He did not make a profit from selling them. Instead, he chose to sell them at a lower price than other stores to attract new customers to Lululemon. Once in the store, they would learn about the yoga-specific clothes Lululemon carried.

A similar technique worked during one of Lululemon's first Christmas seasons. Gray designed a fleece-lined bra that got included in a local magazine's Christmas shopping

> *Lululemon-branded yoga mats are among the many new products the company has introduced over the years.*

TURNING A LEMON INTO LULULEMONADE

In 2002, a batch of fabric did not meet Lululemon's standards. The company recalled all the pants made with the fabric and heavily advertised so customers knew they could exchange the faulty pants. This action helped repair the company's reputation, but now it had 2,000 pairs of pants that it did not know what to do with.[1] Customer feedback had informed Lululemon that women would like to walk their dogs in their yoga pants but did not because the fabric attracted dog hair. Lululemon sewed the faulty fabric into a loose nylon shell and sold it as dog-walking pants. Dog fur did not stick to the nylon. The solution turned out to be a great success, with Lululemon's dog-walking pants becoming a big seller.

guide. Although not a core product, it brought new customers to the store. Once women discovered Lululemon pants or leggings, they were hooked.

One of the things that has set Lululemon apart from its competitors is its frequent introduction of new designs and new products. Because it designs its own products to sell in its own stores, it controls the inventory cycle. Offering new products frequently is one way to draw customers into the store more often. New designs, colors, or technical features are always being introduced.

Lululemon remained focused on yoga wear but started to branch out into new areas, including its first major lines of clothing for children and for men. In 2015, it introduced the ABC men's pant to complement its women's yoga pants. The pants generated a boost in sales and encouraged the company to keep broadening the

> *Adding clothing for men helped the company significantly widen its potential customer base.*

men's line. With men's wear, the company also started to move away from only yoga to include apparel for other sweat-inducing activities, such as cross-training and cycling. It also introduced innovative products, such as Shorts-Your-Way, to appeal to men who engage in a variety of activities. Customers can customize their shorts by selecting from one of four lengths and deciding to add a liner or not.

    In 2017, Lululemon introduced its first marketing initiative directed at men. The "Strength to Be" campaign was a series of five short films about men from different walks of life. The goal of the campaign was to celebrate the growing number of men who were defining masculinity and strength for themselves. By 2019, the men's line accounted for 21 percent of the company's revenue. CEO Calvin McDonald said in the spring of 2019 that he hoped to double revenue from the men's line by 2023.[2]

POP-UP SHOPS

Pop-up shops are small, temporary retail locations set up to introduce new stores and products to local customers. Lululemon uses pop-up shops to test new markets. It opens a pop-up shop in a community where it is planning to open a new store. The shop opens a few days a week to introduce people to Lululemon's clothes. On the days the store is closed, staff use the space to hold yoga or meditation classes or conduct design meetings. Customers are asked to give feedback on the clothes. They are also asked where they want a permanent store. The information gathered from the pop-ups allows Lululemon to confidently invest in opening a new location.

MORE THAN YOGA

As Lululemon's customer base grew, the company started adding more diverse products. Yoga accessories, such as straps, blocks, and water bottles, were natural add-ons. Headbands and no-slip socks could be found by checkout stands. This was followed by a selection of bags ranging from belt bags and cross-body bags to shoppers and backpacks.

Outerwear was also added to the Lululemon line. Initially the company specialized in jackets that were suitable for

THE ABC PANT FOR MEN

PRODUCT SPOTLIGHT

When thinking about growing Lululemon's product lines for the men's market, Wilson knew he had to offer something different from his competitors. He thought about problems with men's clothing. He determined the biggest problem with men's clothes was that pants were uncomfortable. Sitting for long periods of time can leave men constantly adjusting their pants. He began to wonder why he could not design comfortable pants for men just as he had for women. He, too, wanted a pair of pants that stretched and moved and looked good on him.

Wilson ended up developing the ABC Pant for men. Using a four-way stretch fabric it called Warpstreme, Lululemon introduced pants that were comfortable and functional for commuting, working out, and traveling. Introduced in 2015, they were a tremendous hit. They were responsible for a 16 percent increase in sales in a single quarter.[3]

TEAM CANADA BEACH VOLLEYBALL

In 2016, Lululemon won the contract to outfit the Canadian Olympic beach volleyball team for the Olympic Games in Rio de Janeiro, Brazil. Sticking to its formula of placing functionality and fit at the forefront of its designs, the company designed every piece precisely for the athlete wearing it. A 3D body scanner was used to tailor the suits to each athlete's movements and measurements. The suits were tested in a climate simulation chamber that matched the weather in Rio. Lululemon also developed a new high-bonded strap on the women's tops that prevented them from slipping. It was the first time the team had custom-fit uniforms.

spring and fall weather but could also be layered with winter wear. This expanded to include vests, jackets, and coats in a multitude of colors and styles for a wide range of purposes. All jackets and coats are made to the same functional design standards as Lululemon's yoga wear.

In June 2019, Lululemon introduced a gender-neutral self-care line designed by athletes for athletes. Lululemon partnered with Sephora on the initiative. The initial launch included four products available at 50 Lululemon stores, online, and at Sephora stores. Dry shampoo, lip balm, deodorant, and face moisturizers were introduced as products that Lululemon customers needed to transition from gym to street. The line expanded to 17 products by 2021, including hand sanitizer.[4]

Lululemon partnered with the Athletic Propulsion Labs brand of shoes, offering the footwear in some of its stores

> *An ever-widening selection of products in Lululemon stores has helped drive the company's growth over time.*

in 2017. It was a way to test customer reaction to Lululemon selling shoes. In December 2020, the company announced it would be introducing its own line of footwear for release in early 2022. On October 12, 2021, Lululemon was awarded a patent for its planned shoe line.

PROTECTING DESIGNS

In August 2012, Lululemon filed a lawsuit suing Calvin Klein for three patent infringements related to yoga pants. Lululemon claimed elements of the waistband design in its Astro yoga pants were used on Calvin Klein's Performance line of active wear. Calvin Klein pulled its pants from store shelves when the lawsuit was filed. In the end, the case was settled out of court. The settlement terms were never disclosed.

CHAPTER EIGHT

CHALLENGES AND CONTROVERSIES

Lululemon has been a successful brand, but like any business, it has faced challenges and controversies. In 2005, the company was accused of making false claims about the content and functions of a new fabric it introduced called VitaSea. VitaSea was made with a material the company named SeaCell that is made in part from seaweed. Lululemon's labels said VitaSea could reduce stress and detoxify the body. The company also claimed the material had anti-inflammatory and antibacterial benefits. The *New York Times* reported that a test of the material could not find any significant trace of seaweed. The Competition Bureau of Canada said the company was in violation of the nation's Textile Labelling

> *Controversies for Lululemon have centered on not just its products, but also its founder, Chip Wilson.*

Act and ordered Lululemon to remove any label that referenced therapeutic or performance benefits. The act states it is illegal to make false or misleading statements relating to a garment.

Lululemon complied with the order but stood by the fabric. In a press release, the company explained that a complex process was used to make VitaSea, and therefore special testing was required to detect vitamins, minerals, and amino acids in the fabric. Lululemon conducted independent tests that it said confirmed the fabric was consistent with the labeling. Lululemon continues to use VitaSea, but now it promotes only the fabric's softness.

The most publicized controversy Lululemon has faced became known as the see-through pants incident. Lululemon's whole brand is based on quality. It justified its high prices because of the quality of its fabrics and designs. It built a loyal customer base through word of mouth by delivering on the expectations it set for itself. So, in 2013, when customers started complaining about see-through yoga pants, the company's reputation for quality was threatened.

Lululemon acted quickly to put out notices to customers that they should return the pants for a full refund or exchange. The company also pulled all the pants it had made from the same batch of fabric from its stores. This represented 17 percent of its inventory. The company later explained the problem was because of a fault in the manufacturing process but did not offer any details. Its reputation still took a hit. So, too, did its share prices on the stock market. The fiasco cost the company $60 million in sales.[1] Shortly after, Chip Wilson was temporarily invited back to help address the quality control issues. CEO Christine Day resigned a few months later.

> **INDEPENDENT TESTING**
>
> Integrity is a priority at Lululemon. The company stands by all its products and what it claims they can do. To back up these claims, Lululemon engages SGS Company, an independent testing, verification, and certification company based in Switzerland. Before each new season, the company conducts tests on all of Lululemon's products, analyzing them for qualities such as fabric content, pilling, and shrinkage.

RETAIL STUMBLES

Lululemon takes a cautious approach to opening new stores, but not all these endeavors have been successful. A distributor that Wilson worked with at Westbeach named Kano Yamanaka opened a location in Aoyama, Japan, in 2005. Eighteen months later, Lululemon bought out Yamanaka's store. Lululemon then formed a partnership with another Japanese apparel company, Descente, to expand its operations in Asia. It later opened more stores in Japan. But success was not immediate in these markets. The 2008 financial crisis put more pressure on the stores than they could bear, and all six Japanese stores were shuttered that year.

Lululemon faltered again when it tried to enter the children's wear market. In 2009, it introduced stand-alone children's stores, branded as Ivivva. Ivivva carried yoga pants, leggings, crop tops, and hoodies. The clothes were made from the same technical fabrics as Lululemon products, and the company relied on the same community-based outreach to build its customer base. Ivivva stores hosted free yoga and Zumba classes. By 2016, there were 55 Ivivva stores in Canada and the United States. But the success was short-lived. In 2017, Lululemon announced it was closing 40 of its Ivivva stores. And in mid-2020, it shuttered the remaining 15, taking the company out of the children's athletic-wear business.[2] It said at the time that it wanted to focus its attention on other product lines, online sales, and the global market.

Lululemon also tested stand-alone men's stores. It opened a concept store in Manhattan's SOHO

> *An Ivivva store manager sets up one of the Lululemon brand's store showrooms in 2012.*

neighborhood in 2014 and a second one in Toronto in 2016. The stores had table tennis and offered cold-brewed coffee to guests. The concept did not take off. Lululemon decided to stick with stores offering both women's and men's clothing, and it closed the two men's stores in 2019.

In its continuing effort to differentiate itself from its competitors, Lululemon also experimented with lab stores. The first Lululemon lab store opened in Vancouver in 2009. It was a concept store where in-house designers created new products on the spot. They developed smaller collections of the company's latest, most innovative designs to test the market. A second lab store opened in New York City in 2016. However, this concept also failed to thrive. In June 2020, the company closed its lab store in Vancouver.

WORDS MATTER

Wilson had an unusual approach to building a company. His way of doing things worked well in the early days. He surrounded himself with people who thought like him. Everyone who was with Lululemon in the beginning understood and supported Wilson's way of thinking. But as the company grew, the team became bigger and more diverse. Partners and shareholders had more traditional expectations and standards. Wilson did not worry much about what others thought, but this did not work to his or Lululemon's benefit when the company went public.

Wilson always handled his own publicity and media. He was used to speaking for himself and his company. He was not necessarily used to having what he said covered by national or international media. When he said several things that many people found offensive, it had consequences for the company.

In a 2004 interview with *National Post*, a business magazine, Wilson explained that he came up with the name *Lululemon* because the Japanese language does not have an *L*, saying that he thought it was funny to hear Japanese people try to say the name. Many considered the comment racist, and there

ANTI-CAPITALISM HYPOCRISY

In September 2020, Lululemon announced it would be hosting a yoga workshop to "resist capitalism." The session was hosted on Zoom by yoga instructor and Lululemon ambassador Rebby Kern. Participants were told they would learn how "gender constructs across the world have informed culture and the ways violent colonialism has erased these histories to enforce consumerism."[3] However, the company faced backlash from media and the public who noted Lululemon is a multibillion-dollar company built on the capitalist model. Kern, who is a vocal activist in the trans community, was attacked on social media. At the same time, Lululemon was criticized for distancing itself from the workshop's content rather than supporting its ambassador.

were calls for the company to change its name because of these problematic origins. These calls continued into 2021.

Wilson also contributed to the Lululemon blog. He often wrote things that others found questionable. He has expressed a belief that if a child as young as 12 is struggling in school, they should instead be taught a skill and work in a factory. Some also found his comments about women's equality inappropriate. He wrote that he believed that the invention of the birth control pill transformed the lives of couples. He felt it changed the lives of women immediately but that men still wanted women to be like their mothers, and this change led to high divorce rates. The posts were removed from the company website after his departure from the company.

In 2013, when asked by the media about the problem with the batch of see-through pants, he responded by saying, "Quite frankly, some women's bodies just actually don't work. It's about the rubbing through the thighs" and "how much pressure there is."[4] There were instant calls for an apology. A few days later, Wilson did issue a video apology, but most felt he only made things worse. He apologized to Lululemon and its employees for what he had said, not to customers he potentially insulted.

Although Wilson was asked to return to the company to help with quality control after the see-through pants problem, these last comments appeared to be too much for the board of directors. Wilson resigned from the board completely in 2013. He retained the right to designate a board director if he held at least eight percent of the stock. However, the agreement stated this privilege would only be honored if he "did not take any contesting stockholder action."[6] In 2018, Wilson released an autobiography, *Little Black Stretchy Pants*. The book contained information that the Lululemon board felt went against those conditions, and they revoked his right to designate a seat. Wilson publicly disagreed with the decision, but by 2021 he still had no active involvement with the company.

DRAWSTRING MISHAP

In June 2015, Lululemon had to recall 318,000 hoodies, jackets, shirts, and pullovers due to a faulty drawstring. It was made of elastic. When caught on something, it snapped back and hit people in the face. The US Consumer Product Safety Commission reported seven injuries to the face or eye from the elastic drawstrings.[5]

CULTURE OR CULT?

The company's well-documented employee training methods and its community-based approach to customer relations have created a loyal following. This extreme loyalty, combined with Lululemon's unique position in the marketplace as a wellness influencer, also has drawbacks. People sometimes refer to Lululemon as a cult. The culture of the company, the quality of its people, and the development of employees were an integral part of the company from its inception. Wilson credited Lululemon's success to this attention to culture and people above all else. For some, however, this approach was too heavy-handed.

A former employee wrote an article for HuffPost in 2017 that called out Lululemon for its "get fit or die trying" culture. She described the training process as being "indoctrinated into a bottomless pit of groupthink."[7] In the article, she spoke about a working environment that left her feeling worthless if she did not meet Lululemon's authenticity and integrity standards. It was not a flattering description.

In February 2018, Lululemon CEO Laurent Potdevin announced his resignation. Lululemon released a statement saying that Potdevin had not lived up to the company's standards of integrity and respect. No other information was provided. But in an article published by *Racked* the same month, employees complained of a toxic "boy's club culture" at the company.[8] It was reported that the CEO had a relationship with one of the designers. He also hosted drinking parties at the office and chose whom he wanted to join him, making it clear he had favorites. The descriptions of his behavior were contrary to what Lululemon said it stood for.

In 2021, *Insider* interviewed more than a dozen former employees who referred to Lululemon's culture of "toxic positivity." People interviewed described an environment in which putting on a happy face was valued over authenticity. They said they felt the company did not appreciate diverse personality types. They also said racial minorities found it difficult to be heard. It was also noted that most of the people hired were fit, able-bodied, white women. Lululemon

WORKERS' RIGHTS

Lululemon has a strict Vendor Code of Ethics that requires all its manufacturers to follow a single set of policies regardless of local legal or cultural practices. Despite this, the company has faced allegations of using factories that have not adhered to these policies. In 2019, news reports emerged about female workers in a Bangladesh factory alleging they struggled to survive on the wages paid and that they were abused by supervisors. They claimed they were slapped, called names, and forced to work when sick. Lululemon said it would launch an investigation and stopped orders from the factory. In a follow-up report published in February 2020, Lululemon said its investigation "identified findings in line with those that were brought to our attention."[9] It did not provide specifics about any actions or changes resulting from the investigation.

responded to these accusations by saying, "The claims in the *Insider* article are not consistent with the culture and values of Lululemon today."[10] The company also said it encourages feedback, takes it seriously, and takes appropriate action on it.

None of the challenges or controversies seemed to have caused long-term damage to Lululemon. Its sales figures have remained on an upward trend. Despite a few temporary dips in stock price at the height of controversies, the company continued to prosper.

> *In 2018, CEO Laurent Potdevin resigned from Lululemon under circumstances the company declined to make public.*

A BRIGHT FUTURE

Lululemon Athletica plans to stick around. Its goal is not only to become an even bigger player in the athletic wear and athleisure markets but also to continue to grow the company beyond apparel to become a broader wellness and lifestyle brand. Lululemon announced a five-year growth plan in 2019 it called the Power of Three. Its goal was to double its online sales and men's line revenue and quadruple its international revenue by 2023.[1]

By the spring of 2021, the company had already achieved its goal of doubling online revenue.[2] Lululemon was one of the first companies to introduce personal virtual shopping during the pandemic. From the comfort of their homes, customers can

> *In purchasing a company that makes interactive workout mirrors, Lululemon made a significant bet on the future of high-tech fitness.*

MIRROR

In June 2020, Lululemon announced it had purchased at-home fitness start-up company Mirror for $500 million. The company's product is a high-tech, wall-mounted mirror with a camera and a built-in display. Users can take live fitness classes and get one-on-one personal training at home. The mirror is $1,495, and it costs $39 a month to stream classes.[3] The Mirror brand struggled in its first year under Lululemon. Sales failed to meet expectations, and Mirror's CEO resigned in September 2021. The company looked for ways to turn this part of its business around.

get fit and size consultation, product recommendations based on personal needs, and gift suggestions. They can also see a demonstration of Lululemon's new interactive home gym called Mirror. There is an option to choose between a live video chat or off-camera text chatting.

In 2018, the company ran a pilot for a membership program in Edmonton, Alberta, Canada. For an annual fee of $128 Canadian (approximately $100 US), members got benefits like a free pair of pants and free shipping. The experiment was successful enough that Lululemon expanded it to Toronto; Chicago; and Denver, Colorado, by 2021. The annual fee went up to $168 Canadian, and spaces were limited, but the benefits grew. Members had access to exclusive workouts and classes, they received a 20 percent discount on their birthdays, and they got a piece of exclusive gear valued at $100 Canadian. Lululemon used the trials to collect information and get feedback from

> *Like all retailers, Lululemon was forced to make adjustments during the COVID-19 pandemic.*

customers. The membership trial ended in 2021. The company did not say whether it planned to expand on the program.

In its April 2021 fourth-quarter earnings call, Lululemon announced it planned to open between 40 and 50 new stores through 2021 and 2022.[4] It sought to draw more traffic to its stores and cement itself as a lifestyle brand by opening more experiential stores. New stores would also have in-store demos of the Mirror product. The company planned to expand on some of the innovations it adopted during the COVID-19 pandemic, including curbside pickup, virtual wait lists, and shopping by appointment. The company found continued success in late 2021, disclosing in a December earnings call that its year-over-year revenues had increased 30 percent to $1.5 billion.[5]

Lululemon continues to introduce new product lines. It sees no reason why it cannot be the go-to athletic wear and athleisure brand for men just as it has grown to be for women. In addition to expanding its men's line, it will continue to add apparel for other activities, such as cycling and running. In 2021, Lululemon announced it had won the contract to outfit the Canadian Olympic Team from the 2022 Winter Games in Beijing, China, through the 2028 Summer Games in Los Angeles, California. It introduced the Beijing kit in October 2021 and received positive reviews from the athletes for the care and detail put into the designs. In 2020, with people spending more time at home due to the pandemic, the company introduced the On the Move

NO DETAIL MISSED

In 2021, Lululemon was awarded the contract to outfit Canada's Olympic team. The detailed elements included in the clothes highlighted how Lululemon's designers listened to and considered the needs of the athletes. Some of the more thoughtful design elements include a coat that converts from long coat to short jacket to vest. The bottom portion of the coat zips off and turns into a pillow. There is a pocket next to the heart for athletes to keep their medals and even a tiny pocket to hold lip balm.

collection for "working and sweating from home."[6] In 2021, just as in 1998, Lululemon seemed to be able to anticipate what people needed and wanted before its competitors.

A SUSTAINABLE FUTURE

Lululemon says it is interested in a responsible and sustainable future. The company has a vendor code of ethics it requires all suppliers to adhere to. It assesses all potential factories before entering a business relationship and continues to do assessments throughout the duration of contracts. The company has started to trace where its raw materials are sourced. Suppliers are also required to follow the Higg Index 2.0 Facility Environmental Module. The Higg Index is a standard measurement tool that helps suppliers understand

WHITESPACE INNOVATION LAB

Whitespace Innovation Lab was Lululemon's research and development hub. Located in the basement of the company's Vancouver head office, it included between 30 and 50 employees who researched how clothes impacted physical performance. The information collected was used to design better, more functional garments. Treadmills, stationary bikes, an endless pool, a temperature simulation room, heat sensors, 3D printers, and laser cutters were just some of the equipment and technology on hand for employees to test the effectiveness and functionality of their clothing designs. Under pressure from employees who were uncomfortable with the name of the lab, Lululemon's CEO announced in July 2021 it was temporarily shutting down Whitespace. It planned to relaunch under a new name, Lululemon Labs, and a new research and development model.

the environmental impact of the factories they use. If standards are not met, this assessment can be used to develop a plan to improve environmental standards.

In May 2021, Lululemon announced its launch of the Lululemon Like New program. It started in Texas and California, where the company has more than 80 stores combined. Lululemon guests can trade gently used Lululemon clothing for a gift card. All products are cleaned and then made available for resale. Profits from the program are being reinvested into Lululemon's sustainability efforts. The company says purchasing a Lululemon Like New product can save up to 50 percent of the product's carbon footprint.[7]

Lululemon is also working to introduce more sustainable products. In July 2021, it revealed its first three products made from a renewable material called Mylo. Mylo is made from mycelium, a substance in the roots of mushrooms. One of Lululemon's yoga mats is made entirely from Mylo. Two bags feature Mylo in their details. The company sees sustainable innovation as key in its new product development.

> *Like many companies, Lululemon has taken steps to address the issues of sustainability and environmental awareness.*

Lululemon Athletica has no plans to slow down. Just as Chip Wilson envisioned in 1998, the company is on track to become a global health and wellness leader. Compared with its more established competitors, such as Nike and Adidas, it still has a lot of growth potential. There are global markets it has not entered, types of technical athletic wear it has not tackled, and innovative ways of drawing in new customers it has yet to test. Lululemon has plans to take on the challenges of the future as it always has, by engaging and listening to its customers. By responding to customer feedback, Lululemon Athletica intends to stay one step ahead of the next trend.

CENTRE FOR SOCIAL IMPACT

On October 8, 2021, Lululemon announced the launch of its Centre for Social Impact. The Centre's stated purpose was to "disrupt inequity in wellbeing through movement, mindfulness, and advocacy." The company has committed to investing $75 million by 2025 in programs that support physical, mental, and social well-being across all its communities.[8] The Centre's launch initiatives included donations to the Girls Opportunity Alliance, which supports girls' well-being across the globe through education; the National Alliance on Mental Illness, which is dedicated to improving the lives of those living with mental illness; and the Trevor Project, the world's largest suicide-prevention intervention for LGBTQ+ youth.

> *In just a few decades, Lululemon Athletica has used innovative products and the philosophy of its manifesto to change the world of athletic apparel.*

ESSENTIAL FACTS

KEY EVENTS

- Lululemon Athletica is founded by Chip Wilson in 1998 in Vancouver, British Columbia, Canada.

- In March 1999, Lululemon opens its first retail space on West 4th Avenue in Vancouver with six yoga-wear products, including its yoga pants.

- The first Lululemon store opens in the United States in Santa Monica, California, in 2003.

- The first overseas store opens in Melbourne, Australia, in 2004.

- In 2007, Lululemon Athletica goes public, selling 18.2 million shares for $327.6 million.

- On January 29, 2012, Chip Wilson resigns his position as chief innovation and branding officer at Lululemon.

- In 2015, Chip Wilson resigns from the company's board of directors.

KEY PEOPLE

- Chip Wilson is the founder of Lululemon, first CEO, and first chief innovation and branding officer.

- Amanda Dunsmoor is the first designer Chip Wilson hires at Lululemon.

- Shannon (Gray) Wilson is a designer at Lululemon who works on some of its most well-known pieces, such as the Groove Pant.

- Bob Meers, a former Reebok executive, is the first CEO Chip Wilson hires.

- Calvin McDonald becomes CEO in 2018.

KEY PRODUCTS

- Boogie/Groove Pants: The yoga pants that Lululemon is known for, these two designs put Lululemon on the map.

- Leggings: Lululemon's Wunder Unders took leggings from dance classes to yoga. They later became common pieces of street wear around the world.

- Headband: This simple and inexpensive accessory became an instant best-seller. By 2021, there were multiple different styles of headbands.

- ABC Pant: The ABC Pant, introduced in 2015, was one of Lululemon's early moves into the area of men's athletic clothing, a part of the company that grew significantly in the following years.

QUOTE

"Providing components for people to live a longer, healthier, and more fun life."

—*Lululemon's mission statement*

GLOSSARY

ambassador
An individual authorized by an organization or company to represent it or its products.

apparel
A synonym for clothes.

boutique
A small exclusive or specialty shop.

chafe
To make the skin sore by rubbing.

crescent lunge
A yoga pose involving lunging one leg forward and reaching to the sky.

electrolyte
An inorganic compound such as sodium or potassium that plays a role in controlling fluids in the body.

focus group
A group of people selected to evaluate products and give their opinions about them.

gusset
A diamond- or triangular-shaped piece of fabric used in sewing to add extra strength or support to an area of a garment.

manifesto
A written statement that declares one's beliefs, intentions, and goals.

patent
A legal way to protect a product's design from being copied by others.

private equity firm
An investment management company that invests in other businesses.

profit margin
The difference between the cost of making something and the price that a company sells it for.

prototype
A single sample of a prospective product used to show potential customers and investors to gauge their interest.

supply chain
All the people, systems, and businesses that are involved in getting a product from design concept to manufacturing to the consumer.

trademarked
The status of symbols or words being legally protected so that only the owner of the trademark can use them.

ADDITIONAL RESOURCES

SELECTED BIBLIOGRAPHY

Bhasin, Kim, and Gerald Porter Jr. "The Rise of Lululemon: How America Became a Nation of Yoga Pants." *Chicago Tribune*, 31 Oct. 2018, chicagotribune.com. Accessed 24 Nov. 2021.

"History." *Lululemon*, 9 Oct. 2020, info.lululemon.com. Accessed 24 Nov. 2021.

Wilson, Chip. *Little Black Stretchy Pants: The Story of Lululemon.* Time Is Tight Communications, 2018.

FURTHER READINGS

Huddleston, Emma. *Nutrition and Exercise.* Abdo, 2021.

Kallen, Stuart A. *Careers If You Like Sports.* ReferencePoint, 2018.

Streissguth, Tom. *Adidas.* Abdo, 2023.

ONLINE RESOURCES

To learn more about Lululemon Athletica, please visit **abdobooklinks.com** or scan this QR code. These links are routinely monitored and updated to provide the most current information available.

MORE INFORMATION

For more information on this subject, contact or visit the following organizations:

LULULEMON ATHLETICA FLAGSHIP STORE
970 Robson St.
Vancouver, BC, Canada V6Z 2E7
+1 604-681-3118
shop.lululemon.com/stores/ca/vancouver/robson
robson-store@lululemon.com

A major Lululemon store is located in the company's hometown. It is on the same street where Lululemon's second location opened.

YOGA ALLIANCE
1560 Wilson Blvd. #700
Arlington, VA 22209
1-888-921-9642
yogaalliance.org
info@yogaalliance.org

Yoga Alliance is the largest yoga-related nonprofit. It promotes access to yoga, provides professional development for yoga instructors, and encourages safe, equitable practices in the yoga community.

SOURCE NOTES

CHAPTER 1. CLOTHING MADE FOR YOGA

1. Chip Wilson. *Little Black Stretchy Pants: The Story of Lululemon*. Time Is Tight Communications, 2018.
2. Lianne George. "How Lululemon Lost Its Balance." *Maclean's*, 18 Feb. 2008, macleans.ca. Accessed 14 Feb. 2022.
3. "Number of Yoga Participants in the United States." *Statista*, 2022, statista.com. Accessed 14 Feb. 2022.
4. Dani Mackey. "2016 Yoga in America Study Conducted by Yoga Journal and Yoga Alliance Reveals Growth and Benefits of the Practice." *Yoga Alliance*, 13 Jan. 2016, yogaalliance.org. Accessed 14 Feb. 2022.
5. Wilson, *Little Black Stretchy Pants*, 141–143.
6. Wilson, *Little Black Stretchy Pants*, 8.
7. D. Tighe. "Total Number of Lululemon Athletica Stores Worldwide." *Statista*, 12 May 2021, statista.com. Accessed 14 Feb. 2022.
8. "Lululemon Athletica." *Forbes*, 20 Oct. 2021, forbes.com. Accessed 14 Feb. 2022.

CHAPTER 2. FUNCTIONAL FABRIC

1. Sara Lindberg. "Everything You Need to Know about Ironman/Triathlon Distances." *Bicycling*, 4 June 2021, bicycling.com. Accessed 14 Feb. 2022.
2. "Quality Promise." *Lululemon Athletica*, n.d., info.lululemon.com. Accessed 14 Feb. 2022.
3. Chip Wilson. *Little Black Stretchy Pants: The Story of Lululemon*. Time Is Tight Communications, 2018. 136.
4. Kim Bhasin and Ashley Lutz. "Here's What's So Special about Lululemon's 'Luon' Fabric." *Business Insider*, 19 Mar. 2013, businessinsider.com. Accessed 14 Feb. 2022.
5. Wilson, *Little Black Stretchy Pants*, 334.

CHAPTER 3. FUNCTIONAL FASHION

1. Jenni Shepard. "Lululemon Yoga Pants Featured in MoMA Fashion Design Exhibition." *Daily Hive*, 13 Oct. 2017, dailyhive.com. Accessed 14 Feb. 2022.
2. Aileen Lalor. "It's Official: Lululemon Pants Are a Design Classic." *Vancouver Is Awesome*, 23 Oct. 2017, vancouverisawesome.com. Accessed 14 Feb. 2022.
3. "Taking Stock with Teens: Spring 2020 Survey." *Piper Sandler*, 2022, pipersandler.com. Accessed 14 Feb. 2022.
4. "Piper Jaffray 27th Semi-Annual Taking Stock with Teens Survey, Spring 2014." *Piper Sandler*, 2014, pipersandler.com. Accessed 14 Feb. 2022.
5. David Yanofsky. "The US Is Now Buying More Stretchy Pants Than Blue Jeans." *Quartz*, 1 Mar. 2018, qz.com. Accessed 14 Feb. 2022.

CHAPTER 4. RETAIL REIMAGINED

1. Chip Wilson. *Little Black Stretchy Pants: The Story of Lululemon*. Time Is Tight Communications, 2018. 158–160.
2. "Fortune's Fastest Growing Companies: 13. Lululemon Athletica." *Fortune*, 26 Sept. 2011, fortune.com. Accessed 14 Feb. 2022.
3. "Lululemon Athletics Inc., Form 10-K." *Edgar Online*, 22 Mar. 2012, annualreports.com. Accessed 14 Feb. 2022.
4. "Total Number of Lululemon Athletica Stores Worldwide." *Statista*, 12 May 2021, statista.com. Accessed 14 Feb. 2022.
5. "Stores: Lincoln Park." *Lululemon*, 2020, shop.lululemon.com. Accessed 14 Feb. 2022.
6. Marianne Wilson. "The Most Profitable Retailers in Sales per Square Foot Are…" *Chain Store Age*, 31 July 2017, chainstoreage.com. Accessed 14 Feb. 2022.
7. "Sales Value per Square Foot of Selected Department Store Retailers in the United States." *Statista*, 13 Jan. 2022, statista.com. Accessed 14 Feb. 2022.

CHAPTER 5. MORE THAN A BRAND, A CULTURE

1. Chip Wilson. *Little Black Stretchy Pants: The Story of Lululemon*. Time Is Tight Communications, 2018. 8.
2. Wilson, *Little Black Stretchy Pants*, 8.
3. Wilson, *Little Black Stretchy Pants*, 134.
4. Wilson, *Little Black Stretchy Pants*, 8.
5. Fraser Abe. "Lululemon Launches Olympics-timed Line with Worst Name Ever." *Toronto Life*, 15 Dec. 2009, torontolife.com. Accessed 14 Feb. 2022.
6. "Sweat Collective." *Lululemon*, 2022, info.lululemon.com. Accessed 14 Feb. 2022.
7. "Lululemon Collective." *Lululemon*, 2022, shop.lululemon.com. Accessed 14 Feb. 2022.
8. "Lululemon Unveils 'Power of Three' Strategic Plan to Accelerate Growth." *Lululemon*, 24 Apr. 2019, investor.lululemon.com. Accessed 14 Feb. 2022.
9. "Community Carries On." *Lululemon*, 2022, shop.lululemon.com. Accessed 14 Feb. 2022.
10. Wilson, *Little Black Stretchy Pants*, 219–222.

SOURCE NOTES CONTINUED

CHAPTER 6. GROWTH AND CHANGE

1. Chip Wilson. *Little Black Stretchy Pants: The Story of Lululemon*. Time Is Tight Communications, 2018. 262.

2. Anna Hecht. "If You Invested $1000 in Lululemon 10 Years Ago, Here's How Much Money You'd Have Now." *CNBC*, 11 Sep. 2019, cnbc.com. Accessed 14 Feb. 2022.

3. "Lululemon Athletica." *Yahoo Finance*, 2022, finance.yahoo.com. Accessed 14 Feb. 2022.

4. Steve Gelsi. "Lululemon Athletica IPO Jumps 50%." *MarketWatch*, 27 July 2007, marketwatch.com. Accessed 14 Feb. 2022.

5. Glen Korstrom. "International Expansion Key to Lululemon Success." *Business in Vancouver*, 30 Oct. 2018, biv.com. Accessed 14 Feb. 2022.

6. "Total Number of Lululemon Athletica Stores Worldwide." *Statista*, 12 May 2021, statista.com. Accessed 14 Feb. 2022.

7. "100 Fastest Growing Companies." *Fortune*, 2022, fortune.com. Accessed 14 Feb. 2022.

8. "Total Number of Lululemon Athletica Stores Worldwide."

9. Alistair Gray. "Lululemon Plans Overseas Expansion as Yogawear Booms." *Financial Post*, 22 Dec. 2020, financialpost.com. Accessed 14 Feb. 2022.

10. D. Tighe. "Net Revenue of Lululemon Worldwide from 2008 to 2020." *Statista*, 12 May 2021, statista.com. Accessed 14 Feb. 2022.

11. "#574, Chip Wilson." *Forbes*, 2021, forbes.com. Accessed 14 Feb. 2022.

12. Tiffany Hsu. "Lululemon's Chief Executive Resigns over Behavior." *New York Times*, 5 Feb. 2018, nytimes.com. Accessed 14 Feb. 2022.

CHAPTER 7. EXPANDING PRODUCT LINES

1. Chip Wilson. *Little Black Stretchy Pants: The Story of Lululemon*. Time Is Tight Communications, 2018. 211.

2. Lauren Thomas. "Lululemon CEO: 'We Have Very Low Brand Awareness with Men,' but That Business Will Double by 2023." *CNBC*, 24 Apr. 2019, cnbc.com. Accessed 14 Feb. 2022.

3. Adam Gabbatt. "I Wore Lululemon's New Pants—And I Looked like a Dork." *Guardian*, 31 Mar. 2015, theguardian.com. Accessed 14 Feb. 2022.

4. "Selfcare." *Lululemon*, 2022, shop.lululemon.com. Accessed 14 Feb. 2022.

CHAPTER 8. CHALLENGES AND CONTROVERSIES

1. Chip Wilson. *Little Black Stretchy Pants: The Story of Lululemon*. Time Is Tight Communications, 2018. 360.
2. Carla Salpini. "Lululemon to Shutter Ivivva Brand by Mid-2020." *Retail Dive*, 26 Sept. 2019, retaildive.com. Accessed 14 Feb. 2022.
3. Melissa Lopez-Martinez. "Lululemon Faces Backlash for Promoting Workshop to 'Resist Capitalism.'" *CTV News*, 12 Sept. 2020, ctvnews.ca. Accessed 14 Feb. 2022.
4. Lydia Dishman. "Lululemon's Biggest Problem Is a Founder with Foot-in-Mouth Disease." *Forbes*, 8 Nov. 2013, forbes.com. Accessed 14 Feb. 2022.
5. "Tops with Elastic Draw Cords Recalled by Lululemon." *Consumer Product Safety Commission*, 25 June 2015, cpsc.gov. Accessed 14 Feb. 2022.
6. Carter Coudriet. "Lululemon Strips Its Billionaire Founder Chip Wilson of Board-Appointment Power." *Forbes*, 8 May 2019, forbes.com. Accessed 14 Feb. 2022.
7. Elizabeth Licorish. "Lululemon's Cult Culture: Get Fit or Die Trying." *HuffPost*, 6 Dec. 2017, huffpost.com. Accessed 14 Feb. 2022.
8. Chavie Lieber. "Lululemon Employees Report a Toxic 'Boy's Club' Culture." *Racked*, 14 Feb. 2018, racked.com. Accessed 14 Feb. 2022.
9. Joe Lindsey. "The Dark Secrets Lurking Inside Your Outdoor Gear." *Outside*, 21 Feb. 2020, outsideonline.com. Accessed 14 Feb. 2022.
10. Hannah Frishberg. "'Superpositive Lululemon Robot': Staff Call Retailer's Workplace 'Toxic.'" *New York Post*, 13 Apr. 2021, nypost.com. Accessed 14 Feb. 2022.

CHAPTER 9. A BRIGHT FUTURE

1. "Lululemon Unveils 'Power of Three' Strategic Plan to Accelerate Growth." *Lululemon*, 24 Apr. 2019, investor.lululemon.com. Accessed 14 Feb. 2022.
2. Cara Salpini. "Lululemon More Than Doubles E-Commerce in 2020." *Retail Dive*, 31 Mar. 2021, retaildive.com. Accessed 14 Feb. 2022.
3. Lauren Thomas. "Lululemon to Acquire At-Home Fitness Company Mirror for $500 Million." *CNBC*, 29 June 2020, cnbc.com. Accessed 14 Feb. 2022.
4. Luis Sanchez. "Lululemon's New Experimental Store Hints at the Future of Retail." *Motley Fool*, 23 July 2019, fool.com. Accessed 14 Feb. 2022.
5. Abigail Gentrup. "Lululemon Revenue Up Despite Mirror's Struggles." *Front Office Sports*, 10 Dec. 2021, frontofficesports.com. Accessed 14 Feb. 2022.
6. John Ballard. "Where Will Lululemon Be in 5 Years?" *Motley Fool*, 13 Nov. 2020, fool.com. Accessed 14 Feb. 2022.
7. "Introducing Lululemon Like New." *Lululemon*, 4 May 2021, info.lululemon.com. Accessed 14 Feb. 2022.
8. "Lululemon Launches Centre for Social Impact to Further Advance Equity in Wellbeing." *Businesswire*, 8 Oct. 2021, businesswire.com. Accessed 14 Feb. 2022.

INDEX

ABC Pant for Men, 73
Adidas, 6, 52, 98
advertising, 42, 53, 70
ambassador program, 8, 54, 56, 83
athleisure, 28

Boogie Pant, 29, 30

Calvin Klein, 75
Centre for Social Impact, 98
company name, 10, 83–84
corporate culture, 47–57, 65, 66, 85–89
COVID-19 pandemic, 61, 93

Day, Christine, 65–67, 79
dog-walking pants, 70
Dunsmoor, Amanda, 25, 37, 48

employee development, 48–52
experiential stores, 36, 43, 93

Gap, The, 60
grassroots growth, 38, 42, 52
Gray, Shannon, 31, 32, 48, 69
Groove Pant, 32

Hon, Frankie and Elky, 21

initial public offering, 61–62, 65
Ironman competition, 13–14, 19
Ivivva, 80

Japan, 27, 62, 64, 79–80, 83

Kern, Rebby, 83

Little Black Stretchy Pants, 85
Liz Claiborne, 60
logo, 21
London, England, 62–63
Lululemon Collective, 54–56
Lululemon lab stores, 82
Lululemon Like New, 97
Luon fabric, 19

manifesto, 10, 47, 53, 56–57, 63
McDonald, Calvin, 64, 67, 72
Meers, Bob, 65, 67
Melbourne, Australia, 62
membership program, 92–93
men's clothing, 33, 70–72, 73, 80–82, 91, 94
Mirror, 92, 93
mission statement, 47
Museum of Modern Art, 29
Mylo fabric, 97

National Alliance on Mental Illness, 98
Nike, 6, 52, 98

Olympics, 53, 74, 94
online shopping, 64, 65, 74, 80, 91

pop-up shops, 40, 62–63, 72
Potdevin, Laurent, 67, 86
product recalls, 70, 85
product testing, 78, 79

quality guarantee, 15

Schweitzer, Deanne, 65
Schweitzer, Delaney, 65
see-through pants incident, 78–79, 84–85
Sephora, 67, 74
shopping bags, 53, 56–57
Singapore, 63
Slater, Jackie, 48
stores, 8, 21, 27, 28, 35–45, 52, 61, 62–64, 69–70, 72, 79–82, 93
supply chains, 35
sustainability, 95–97
Sweat Collective, 54

Team Canada, 74, 94
technical fabric, 14, 16, 80
Times Square, 61
Toronto, Canada, 39, 82, 92
Tracy, Brian, 48
Trevor Project, 98

Vancouver, Canada, 8–9, 15, 29, 36, 37, 38, 39, 40, 57, 82, 95
vertical retail, 35–36, 45
Victoria's Secret, 59
VitaSea fabric, 77–78

Warpstreme, 73
Westbeach Snowboard, 8, 17, 21, 25, 36, 48, 79
Whitespace Innovation Lab, 95
wicking fabric, 6, 16, 18, 23, 30
Wilson, Chip, 8–10, 13–21, 25, 27–32, 35–41, 47–52, 54, 57, 59–60, 62, 65–67, 73, 79, 82–85
workers' rights, 87
Wunder Unders, 30

yoga, 5–9, 14–18, 22–23, 28, 30, 37–39, 43, 53, 56, 62, 83
yoga instructors, 15, 16–17, 38, 54, 83
yoga mats, 39, 69, 97

ABOUT THE AUTHOR

RACQUEL FORAN

Racquel Foran is a freelance writer from Coquitlam, British Columbia, Canada. She has authored several nonfiction titles for school-age readers covering diverse subjects, including organ transplants, robotics, eating disorders, and more. When she isn't writing, Foran enjoys tending to her Little Free Library, painting, and walking her dogs in the forest.

ABOUT THE CONSULTANT

JOHN MEINDL

Professor John Meindl is a lecturer of sport management at Farmingdale State College (SUNY) and an adjunct assistant professor of marketing and international business at Hofstra University. He has taught sports business at the undergraduate and graduate levels since 2003. Mr. Meindl is also the founder and CEO of SPORTSBRANDEDMEDIA, INC., a convergence of sport and entertainment. A thought leader in sports marketing, he is an industry pioneer, creating ideas and solutions to meet the challenges of today's changing sports landscape. Mr. Meindl has been a strong advocate for inner-city and underprivileged youth and likes "using sports to include the excluded."